D1294476

# ALL AROUND THE WORLD
# COSTA RICA

by Kristine Spanier, MLIS

pogo

# Ideas for Parents and Teachers

Pogo Books let children practice reading informational text while introducing them to nonfiction features such as headings, labels, sidebars, maps, and diagrams, as well as a table of contents, glossary, and index.

Carefully leveled text with a strong photo match offers early fluent readers the support they need to succeed.

## Before Reading

- "Walk" through the book and point out the various nonfiction features. Ask the student what purpose each feature serves.
- Look at the glossary together. Read and discuss the words.

## Read the Book

- Have the child read the book independently.
- Invite him or her to list questions that arise from reading.

## After Reading

- Discuss the child's questions. Talk about how he or she might find answers to those questions.
- Prompt the child to think more. Ask: Protecting the environment is important to the people of Costa Rica. What do you do to protect the environment?

Pogo Books are published by Jump!
5357 Penn Avenue South
Minneapolis, MN 55419
www.jumplibrary.com

Copyright © 2021 Jump!
International copyright reserved in all countries. No part of this book may be reproduced in any form without written permission from the publisher.

Library of Congress Cataloging-in-Publication Data

Names: Spanier, Kristine, author.
Title: Costa Rica / by Kristine Spanier.
Description: Minneapolis: Jump!, [2021]
Series: All around the world | Includes index.
Audience: Ages 7-10 | Audience: Grades 2-3
Identifiers: LCCN 2019036705 (print)
LCCN 2019036706 (ebook)
ISBN 9781645273295 (hardcover)
ISBN 9781645273301 (paperback)
ISBN 9781645273318 (ebook)
Subjects: LCSH: Costa Rica—Juvenile literature.
Classification: LCC F1543.2 .S63 2021 (print) | LCC F1543.2 (ebook) | DDC 972.86—dc23
LC record available at https://lccn.loc.gov/2019036705
LC ebook record available at https://lccn.loc.gov/2019036706

Editor: Jenna Gleisner
Designer: Molly Ballanger

Photo Credits: Bos11/Shutterstock, cover; ad_foto/iStock, 1; Pixfiction/Shutterstock, 3; riekephotos/Shutterstock, 4t; Julio Salgado/Shutterstock, 4b; Inspired By Maps/Shutterstock, 5; Esdelval/Shutterstock, 6-7; stellamc/Shutterstock, 8-9; Pawel Toczynski/Getty, 10; kjorgen/iStock, 11; Sanit Fuangnakhon/Shutterstock, 12; Kevin Wells/iStock, 12-13; Divepic/iStock, 14-15; Timmary/Shutterstock, 16l; bergamont/Shutterstock, 16r; Jorge A. Russell/Shutterstock, 17; Eyal Nahmias/Alamy, 18-19; Cara Koch/Shutterstock, 20-21; Janusz Pienkowski/Shutterstock, 23.

Printed in the United States of America at Corporate Graphics in North Mankato, Minnesota.

# TABLE OF CONTENTS

# CHAPTER 1

# WELCOME TO COSTA RICA!

See a purple and orange crab on the beach. Or spot leatherback turtles! They are born on the beaches here. Welcome to Costa Rica!

crab

leatherback turtle

See more than 300 large stone spheres. They are more than 1,000 years old. What were they used for? It is a mystery!

sphere

Arenal
Volcano ·····▶

More than 200 **volcanoes** are here. Arenal Volcano is still **active**. The water nearby is heated underground by the volcano. This creates **hot springs**.

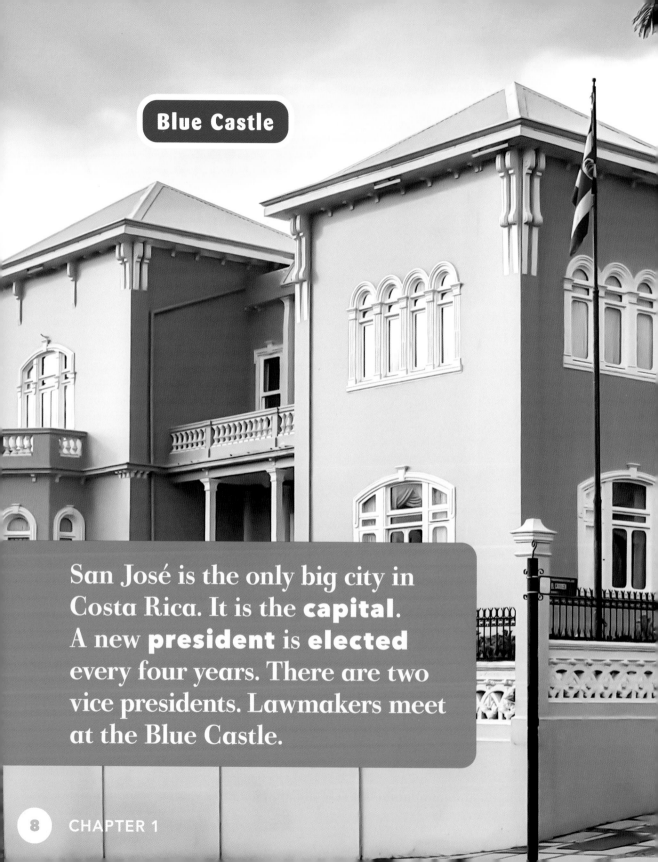

**Blue Castle**

San José is the only big city in Costa Rica. It is the **capital**. A new **president** is **elected** every four years. There are two vice presidents. Lawmakers meet at the Blue Castle.

# TAKE A LOOK!

San José shares a name with the **province** it is in. Costa Rica has seven provinces.

**PROVINCES:**
1. Guanacaste
2. Alajuela
3. Heredia
4. San José
5. Cartago
6. Limón
7. Puntarenas

# CHAPTER 2

# A COUNTRY OF FORESTS

Mount Chirripó ·····▶

Many kinds of forests cover this country. **Tropical** rain forests cover the Talamanca Mountains. Mount Chirripó is the highest point. It is 12,533 feet (3,820 meters) high.

Spider monkeys live in rain forest trees. Jaguars prowl the forest floor.

spider monkey

Cloud forests are covered in mist. This is from cooling air from nearby mountains.

Elfin woodlands have short trees. They are draped in **air plants**. Moss covers the ground.

air plant

cloud forest

scalloped
hammerhead shark

coral reef

Cocos Island is 342 miles (550 kilometers) from the mainland. **Coral reefs** are in the water. The scalloped hammerhead shark swims in the water. The silky shark does, too.

## DID YOU KNOW?

Cocos Island is a national park. The government protects the land. In the early 1980s, a warming event destroyed much of the coral reefs here. They are still recovering. The government works to protect them. Visitors are limited.

# CHAPTER 3

# COSTA RICA'S PEOPLE

Costa Ricans farm many **crops**. Coffee is the oldest **export** here. But now bananas are the largest export. Pineapples and sugar are also exports.

coffee beans

On weekends, people head to the beautiful beaches. You might see surfers!

uniform

The government makes sure all children can go to school. Families get free books if they need them. Students start school at age six. They attend until they are 16. They wear uniforms.

**WHAT DO YOU THINK?**

Costa Rica does not have an army. It stays **neutral**. Do you think your government should be neutral? Why or why not?

Independence Day is September 15. People go to parades. There are also parades before Easter.

Art and celebration are a big part of life here. Artists paint wood carvings and oxcarts.

Costa Rica is a land of wonder. Would you like to visit?

## WHAT DO YOU THINK?

People here say, "pura vida." It means "pure life." It is a way to say hello. It is also a way to show respect. How do you greet others?

Independence Day parade

# QUICK FACTS & TOOLS

## COSTA RICA

**Location:** Central America

**Size:** 19,730 square miles (51,100 square kilometers)

**Population:** 4,987,142 (July 2018 estimate)

**Capital:** San José

**Type of Government:** presidential republic

**Languages:** Spanish and English

**Exports:** bananas, pineapples, coffee, sugar, beef

**Currency:** Costa Rican colón

# GLOSSARY

**active:** An active volcano is one that has had at least one eruption within the past 10,000 years.

**air plants:** Tropical plants that grow on trees and have long, narrow leaves that absorb water and nutrients from the air.

**capital:** A city where government leaders meet.

**coral reefs:** Strips of coral close to the surface of the ocean or another body of water.

**crops:** Plants grown for food.

**elected:** Chosen for office by votes.

**export:** A product sold to different countries.

**hot springs:** Natural sources of hot water that flow from the ground.

**neutral:** Not supporting or agreeing with either side of a disagreement.

**president:** The leader of a country.

**province:** A district or a region in a country.

**tropical:** Of or having to do with the hot, rainy area of the tropics.

**volcanoes:** Mountains with openings through which molten lava, ash, and hot gases erupt.

Costa Rica's currency

## INDEX

## TO LEARN MORE

Finding more information is as easy as 1, 2, 3.

① Go to www.factsurfer.com

② Enter "CostaRica" into the search box.

③ Click the "Surf" button to see a list of websites.

FACT SURFER